The Roller Coaster Ride

Les Howard

Illustrated by Rick Faust

Dominie Press, Inc.

The development of the *Carousel Readers* was supported by the Reading Recovery project at California State University, San Bernardino. All authors' royalties from the sale of the *Carousel Readers* will be used to support various Reading Recovery projects.

Publisher: Raymond Yuen
Illustrator: Rick Faust
Cover Designer: Pamela Pettigrew-Norquist

Copyright © 1995 Dominie Press, Inc.

All rights reserved. No part of this publication may be reproduced or transmitted in any form or by any means without permission in writing from the publisher. Reproduction of any part of this book, through photocopy, recording, or any electronic or mechanical retrieval system, without the written permission of the publisher is an infringement of the copyright law.

Published by

Dominie Press, Inc.
5945 Pacific Center Boulevard
San Diego, California 92121 USA

ISBN 1-56270-373-0
Printed in Singapore by PH Productions.

2 3 4 5 6 7 PH 98 97 96 95

We went to the amusement park.
There were so many people
I had to hold Mom's hand.

Mom got a ticket for the roller coaster.
We sat in the first car.
Mom said, "This is going to be fun."

At first we went slow.
Mom held my hand
so I would not get scared.
We went very high and
then we went . . .

... very, very fast.
We zoomed down and then we zoomed up.

We zoomed this way,
and we zoomed that way.
We zoomed under,
and we zoomed over.
We screamed and we yelled.

When we stopped I said,
"That was fun!"
Mom didn't say anything.